# Pocket Shawls

Featuring pockets and sometimes a hood, these shawls are true comfort fashions! Each is sized for adult and child, and two include doll size.

LEISURE ARTS, INC. • Maumelle, Arkansas

# COASTAL TIDE

 **EASY**

## SHOPPING LIST

**Yarn** (Medium Weight)

[3.5 ounces, 270 yards
(100 grams, 247 meters) per skein]:

☐ 3{4} skeins

### Crochet Hook

☐ Size I (5.5 mm)

**or** size needed for gauge

### Additional Supplies

☐ Pins

## SIZE INFORMATION

**Finished Size:**

12½" wide x 55{75}" long
[32 cm x 139.5{190.5} cm]

*Size Note:* We have printed the
instructions for the sizes in different
colors to make it easier for you to find:
• Child size in Blue
• Adult size in Pink
Instructions in Black apply to both
sizes.

## GAUGE INFORMATION

One repeat = 4" (10 cm) (from point
to point); 10 rows = 4¼" (10.75 cm)

**Gauge Swatch:** 12" wide x 4¼" long
(30.5 cm x 10.75 cm)

Work same as Body for 10 rows: 51 sc.

## INSTRUCTIONS
## Body

Ch 54.

**Row 1** (Right side)**:** Working in
back ridge of beginning ch *(Fig. 1,
page 29)*, dc in fourth ch from hook
**(3 skipped chs count as first dc, now
and throughout)**, 2 dc in each of next
2 chs, skip next ch, (dc in next ch, skip
next ch) 5 times, ★ 2 dc in each of
next 6 chs, skip next ch, (dc in next ch,
skip next ch) 5 times; repeat from ★
once **more**, 2 dc in each of last 3 chs:
51 dc.

*Note:* Loop a short piece of yarn
around any stitch to mark Row 1 as
**right** side.

**Row 2:** Ch 1, turn; sc in each dc
across.

**Row 3:** Ch 3 **(counts as first dc, now
and throughout)**, turn; working in
Back Loops Only *(Fig. 3, page 29)*,
dc in first sc, 2 dc in each of next 2 sc,
skip next sc, (dc in next sc, skip next
sc) 5 times, ★ 2 dc in each of next 6 sc,
skip next sc, (dc in next sc, skip next
sc) 5 times; repeat from ★ once **more**,
2 dc in each of last 3 sc.

**Row 4:** Ch 1, turn; sc in both loops of
each dc across.

Repeat Rows 3 and 4 for pattern
until Body measures approximately
55{75}"/139.5{190.5} cm from
beginning ch at lowest point, ending
by working Row 4.

Finish off.

**First Side Trim:** With **right** side facing
and working from **left** to **right**, join
yarn with slip st in last dc at end of
Row 1; work reverse sc evenly
across ends of rows *(Figs. 6a-d,
page 30)*; finish off.

**Second Side Trim:** With **right** side
facing and working from **left** to **right**,
join yarn with slip st in last sc at end
of last row; work reverse sc evenly
across ends of rows; finish off.

## Pocket (Make 2)

Ch 37.

**Row 1** (Right side): Working in back ridge of beginning ch, dc in fourth ch from hook, 2 dc in each of next 2 chs, skip next ch, (dc in next ch, skip next ch) 5 times, 2 dc in each of next 6 chs, skip next ch, (dc in next ch, skip next ch) 5 times, 2 dc in each of last 3 chs: 34 dc.

*Note:* Mark Row 1 as **right** side.

**Row 2:** Ch 1, turn; sc in each dc across.

**Row 3:** Ch 3, turn; working in Back Loops Only, dc in first sc, 2 dc in each of next 2 sc, skip next sc, (dc in next sc, skip next sc) 5 times, 2 dc in each of next 6 sc, skip next sc, (dc in next sc, skip next sc) 5 times, 2 dc in each of last 3 sc.

**Row 4:** Ch 1, turn; sc in both loops of each dc across.

Repeat Rows 3 and 4 until piece measures approximately 10" (25.5 cm) from beginning ch at lowest point, ending by working Row 4.

Finish off.

Using photo as a guide for placement, pin Pockets at hand level when worn, leaving top edge of Pocket open. Join yarn with slip st at one side edge, slip st around pinned sides of each Pocket; finish off.

3

# PERKY PATCHES

◼◼◼◻ INTERMEDIATE

## SHOPPING LIST

### Yarn (Medium Weight)

[3.5 ounces, 170 yards
(100 grams, 156 meters) per skein]:

- ☐ Dk Gold - 6{7} skeins
- ☐ Red - 1 skein
- ☐ Rust - 1 skein
- ☐ Beige - 1 skein
- ☐ Gold - 1 skein

### Crochet Hook

- ☐ Size H (5 mm)
  **or** size needed for gauge

### Additional Supplies

- ☐ Pins
- ☐ Yarn needle

## SIZE INFORMATION

**Finished Size:**

12¼" (31 cm) wide x 22{36}"
[56{91.5} cm] long (from inside
center back neck to bottom edge)

*Size Note:* We have printed the
instructions for the sizes in different
colors to make it easier for you to find:

- Child size in Blue
- Adult size in Pink

Instructions in Black apply to both
sizes.

## GAUGE INFORMATION

15 linked dc and 8 rows = 4" (10 cm)
**Gauge Swatch:** 12" wide x 4" long (30.5 cm x 10 cm)
Work same as Long Strip, page 6, for 8 rows: 45 linked dc.

## ─── STITCH GUIDE ───

🎥 **BEGINNING LINKED DOUBLE CROCHET** *(abbreviated beginning linked dc)*

Insert hook in second ch from hook, YO and pull up a loop, insert hook in first
linked dc, YO and pull up a loop (3 loops on hook), (YO and draw through
2 loops on hook) twice.

🎥 **LINKED DOUBLE CROCHET** *(abbreviated linked dc)*

Insert hook in horizontal bar of previous linked dc *(Fig. A)*, YO and pull up a loop,
insert hook in next st, YO and pull up a loop (3 loops on hook) *(Fig. B)*, (YO and
draw through 2 loops on hook) twice *(Fig. C)*.

**Fig. A**

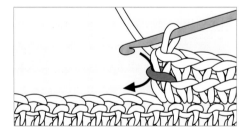

**Fig. B**

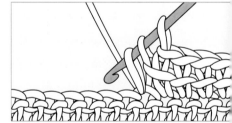

**Fig. C**

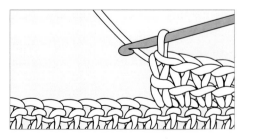

## INSTRUCTIONS
## Long Strip

With Dk Gold, ch 47.

**Row 1** (Right side)**:** Insert hook in second ch from hook, YO and pull up a loop, insert hook in next ch, YO and pull up a loop (3 loops on hook), (YO and draw through 2 loops on hook) twice (**counts as first linked dc**), work linked dc across: 45 linked dc.

*Note:* Loop a short piece of yarn around any stitch to mark Row 1 as **right** side.

**Row 2:** Ch 2, turn; work beginning linked dc, work linked dc across.

Repeat Row 2 for pattern until Long Strip measures approximately 33¾{47¾}"/85.5{121.5} cm from beginning ch, ending by working a **right** side row.

Finish off.

## Short Strip

Work same as Long Strip until Short Strip measures approximately 21¾{35¾}"/55{91} cm from beginning ch, ending by working a **right** side row.

Finish off.

Using Diagram as a guide for placement, working through **both** loops of each ch on Short Strip and in ends of rows on Long Strip, 📹 whipstitch (*Fig. 5a, page 30)* Strips together.

### Diagram

┌─ 21¾{35¾}" ─┐
│ Short Strip │ (12")
└─ 22{36}" ─┘
Long Strip — 33¾{47¾}"

*Note:* Schematic measurements are before Trim.

## Pocket (Make 2)
## SQUARE

(Make one **each** in Red, Rust, Beige, **and** Gold)

Ch 17.

**Row 1** (Right side)**:** Insert hook in second ch from hook, YO and pull up a loop, insert hook in next ch, YO and pull up a loop (3 loops on hook), (YO and draw through 2 loops on hook) twice (**counts as first linked dc**), work linked dc across: 15 linked dc.

*Note:* Mark Row 1 as **right** side **and** bottom edge.

**Rows 2-7:** Ch 2, turn; work beginning linked dc, work linked dc across.

Finish off.

Using photo as a guide for placement, hold 2 Squares with **wrong** sides together, matching bottom edge of one Square to top edge of second Square. Using matching color, sew Squares together, forming 2 strips of 2 Squares each, beginning in first corner and ending in next corner; then sew strips together in same manner.

## EDGING

**Rnd 1:** With **right** side of Pocket facing,  join Dk Gold with sc in any corner *(see Joining With Sc, page 29)*; 2 sc in same st, ★ work 26 sc evenly spaced across to next corner, 3 sc in corner; repeat from ★ 2 times **more**; work 26 sc evenly spaced across; join with slip st to first sc: 116 sc.

**Rnd 2:** Ch 1, do **not** turn; sc in same sc as joining, 3 sc in next corner sc, ★ sc in each sc across to center sc of next corner 3-sc group, 3 sc in center sc; repeat from ★ 2 times **more**, sc in each sc across; join with slip st to first sc, finish off.

Using photo as a guide for placement, place bottom edge of each Pocket approximately 1" (2.5 cm) from bottom edge of each Strip, centering Pocket across the width. Pin Pockets in place. With Dk Gold, sew around three sides of each Pocket, leaving top edge of Pocket open.

**Trim:** With **right** side facing, join Red with sc in any st; sc evenly around entire piece working 3 sc in each corner; repeat from ★ once **more**; join with slip st to first sc, finish off.

# GRANNY POCKETS

**━━◼◻◻ EASY**

## SHOPPING LIST

### Yarn (Medium Weight)

[4 ounces, 200 yards
(113 grams, 183 meters) per skein]:
☐ Grey - 4{5} skeins

[5 ounces, 251 yards
(142 grams, 230 meters) per skein]:
☐ Rust - 1 skein

### Crochet Hook
☐ Size J (6 mm)
**or** size needed for gauge

### Additional Supplies
☐ Pins
☐ Yarn needle

## SIZE INFORMATION

**Finished Size:**
12" wide x 55{70}" long
[30.5 cm x 139.5{178} cm]

*Size Note:* We have printed the
instructions for the sizes in different
colors to make it easier for you to find:
• Child size in Blue
• Adult size in Pink
Instructions in Black apply to both
sizes.

## GAUGE INFORMATION

In pattern, 12 sts (4 3-dc groups) and
7 rows = 4" (10 cm)

**Gauge Swatch:** 4½" wide x 4" long
(11.5 cm x 10 cm)

With Grey, ch 16.
Work same as Body for 7 rows:
4 3-dc groups.
Finish off.

## INSTRUCTIONS
## Body

Each row is worked across the length
of the Shawl.

With Grey, ch 166{211}.

**Row 1** (Right side)**:** 3 Dc in fifth ch
from hook (**4 skipped chs count as
first dc and one skipped ch**), ★ skip
next 2 chs, 3 dc in next ch; repeat
from ★ across to last 2 chs, skip next
ch, dc in last ch: 54{69} 3-dc groups.

*Note:* Loop a short piece of yarn
around any stitch to mark Row 1 as
**right** side.

**Row 2:** Ch 3 (**counts as first dc,
now and throughout**), turn; 2 dc in
🎥 sp **before** next 3-dc group *(Fig. 4,
page 30)*, ★ skip next 3-dc group, 3 dc
in sp **before** next 3-dc group; repeat
from ★ across to last 4 dc, skip next
3-dc group, 2 dc in sp **before** last dc,
dc in last dc: 53{68} 3-dc groups.

**Row 3:** Ch 3, turn; skip next 2 dc, 3 dc
in sp **before** next 3-dc group, ★ skip
next 3-dc group, 3 dc in sp **before**
next 3-dc group; repeat from ★ across
to last 3-dc group, skip next 2 dc, dc
in last dc: 54{69} 3-dc groups.

**Row 4:** Ch 3, turn; 2 dc in sp **before**
next 3-dc group, ★ skip next
3-dc group, 3 dc in sp **before** next
3-dc group; repeat from ★ across to
last 4 dc, skip next 3-dc group, 2 dc
in sp **before** last dc, dc in last dc:
53{68} 3-dc groups.

Repeat Rows 3 and 4 for pattern until
Body measures approximately 12"
(30.5 cm) from beginning ch, ending
by working Row 3.

**Edging:** Ch 1, do **not** turn; sc evenly
around entire piece working 3 sc in
each corner; join with slip st to first sc
finish off.

## First Pocket

### SQUARE (Make 4)

With Rust, ch 5; join with slip st to form a ring.

**Rnd 1** (Right side)**:** Ch 3, 2 dc in ring, ch 2, (3 dc in ring, ch 2) 3 times; join with slip st to first dc, finish off: 12 dc and 4 ch-2 sps.

*Note:* Mark Rnd 1 as **right** side.

**Rnd 2:** With **right** side facing, 🎥 join Grey with dc in any ch-2 sp *(see Joining With Dc, page 29)*; (2 dc, ch 2, 3 dc) in same sp, ch 1, ★ (3 dc, ch 2, 3 dc) in next ch-2 sp, ch 1; repeat from ★ 2 times **more**; join with slip st to first dc, finish off: 24 dc and 8 sps.

**Rnd 3:** With **right** side facing, join Rust with dc in any corner ch-2 sp; (2 dc, ch 2, 3 dc) in same sp, ch 1, 3 dc in next ch-1 sp, ch 1, ★ (3 dc, ch 2, 3 dc) in next corner ch-2 sp, ch 1, 3 dc in next ch-1 sp, ch 1; repeat from ★ 2 times **more**; join with slip st to first dc, do **not** finish off: 36 dc and 12 sps.

**Rnd 4:** Ch 1, sc in same st as joining, sc in each dc and in each ch-1 sp around working 3 sc in each corner ch-2 sp; join with slip st to first sc, finish off: 56 sc.

With **wrong** sides together and Grey, working through **inside** loops of **both** pieces, 🎥 whipstitch Squares together *(Fig. 5b, page 30)*, forming 2 strips of 2 Squares each, beginning in center sc of first corner 3-sc group and ending in center sc of next corner 3-sc group; then whipstitch Strips together in same manner.

### EDGING

**Rnd 1:** With **right** side facing, 🎥 join Grey with sc in center sc of any corner 3-sc group *(see Joining With Sc, page 29)*; 2 sc in same st, ★ sc in each sc across to center sc of next corner 3-sc group, 3 sc in center sc; repeat from ★ 2 times **more**, sc in each sc across; join with slip st to first sc.

**Rnd 2:** Ch 1, sc in same st as joining, 3 sc in next corner sc, ★ sc in each sc across to center sc of next corner 3-sc group, 3 sc in center sc; repeat from ★ 2 times **more**, sc in each sc across; join with slip st to first sc, finish off.

## Second Pocket

With Rust, ch 5; join with slip st to form a ring.

**Rnd 1** (Right side)**:** Ch 3, 2 dc in ring, ch 2, ★ 3 dc in ring, ch 2; repeat from ★ 2 times **more**; join with slip st to first dc; do **not** finish off: 12 dc and 4 ch-2 sps.

*Note:* Mark Rnd 1 as **right** side.

**Rnd 2:** Slip st in next 2 dc and in next ch-2 sp, ch 3, (2 dc, ch 2, 3 dc) in same sp, ch 1, ★ (3 dc, ch 2, 3 dc) in next ch-2 sp, ch 1; repeat from ★ 2 times **more**; join with slip st to first dc: 24 dc and 8 sps.

**Rnd 3:** Slip st in next 2 dc and in next corner ch-2 sp, ch 3, (2 dc, ch 2, 3 dc) in same sp, ch 1, 3 dc in next ch-1 sp, ch 1, ★ (3 dc, ch 2, 3 dc) in next corner ch-2 sp, ch 1, 3 dc in next ch-1 sp, ch 1; repeat from ★ 2 times **more**; join with slip st to first dc, finish off: 36 dc and 12 sps.

**Rnd 4:** With **right** side facing, join Grey with dc in any corner ch-2 sp; (2 dc, ch 2, 3 dc) in same sp, ch 1, (3 dc in next ch-1 sp, ch 1) twice, ★ (3 dc, ch 2, 3 dc) in next corner ch-2 sp, ch 1, (3 dc in next ch-1 sp, ch 1) twice; repeat from ★ 2 times **more**; join with slip st to first dc: 48 dc and 16 sps.

**Rnd 5:** Slip st in next 2 dc and in next corner ch-2 sp, ch 3, (2 dc, ch 2, 3 dc) in same sp, ch 1, ★ (3 dc in next ch-1 sp, ch 1) 3 times, (3 dc, ch 2, 3 dc) in next corner ch-2 sp, ch 1; repeat from ★ 2 times **more**, (3 dc in next ch-1 sp, ch 1) 3 times; join with slip st to first dc, finish off: 60 dc and 20 sps.

**Rnd 6:** With **right** side facing, join Rust with dc in any corner ch-2 sp; (2 dc, ch 2, 3 dc) in same sp, ch 1, ★ (3 dc in next ch-1 sp, ch 1) 4 times, (3 dc, ch 2, 3 dc) in next corner ch-2 sp, ch 1; repeat from ★ 2 times **more**, (3 dc in next ch-1 sp, ch 1) 4 times; join with slip st to first dc: 72 dc and 24 sps.

**Rnd 7:** Slip st in next 2 dc and in next corner ch-2 sp, ch 3, (2 dc, ch 2, 3 dc) in same sp, ch 1, ★ (3 dc in next ch-1 sp, ch 1) 5 times, (3 dc, ch 2, 3 dc) in next corner ch-2 sp, ch 1; repeat from ★ 2 times **more**, (3 dc in next ch-1 sp, ch 1) 5 times; join with slip st to first dc, finish off: 84 dc and 28 sps.

**Rnd 8:** With **right** side facing, join Grey with sc in any corner ch-2 sp; 2 sc in same sp, ★ sc in each dc and in each ch-1 sp across to next corner ch-2 sp, 3 sc in corner ch-2 sp; repeat from ★ 2 times **more**, sc in each dc and in each ch-1 sp across; join with slip st to first sc: 120 sc.

**Rnd 9:** Ch 1, sc in same st as joining, 3 sc in next corner sc, ★ sc in each sc across to center sc of next corner 3-sc group, 3 sc in center sc; repeat from ★ 2 times **more**, sc in each sc across; join with slip st to first sc, finish off: 128 sc.

Using photo as a guide for placement, page 9, place bottom edge of each Pocket approximately 1" (2.5 cm) from bottom edge of each end of Strip, centering Pocket across the width. Pin Pockets in place. Sew around three sides of each Pocket, leaving top edge of Pockets open.

# HOODED COMFY

 ●●□□ **EASY**

## SHOPPING LIST

### Yarn (Medium Weight) 🅴4

[3.5 ounces, 207 yards
(100 grams, 188 meters) per skein]:
☐ 4{5} skeins

### Crochet Hook

☐ Size H (5 mm)
**or** size needed for gauge

### Additional Supplies

☐ Pins
☐ Yarn needle

## SIZE INFORMATION

**Finished Size:**
12" wide x 55{70}" long
[30.5 cm x 139.5{178} cm]

*Size Note:* We have printed the instructions for the sizes in different colors to make it easier for you to find:
• Child size in Blue
• Adult size in Pink
Instructions in Black apply to both sizes.

## GAUGE INFORMATION

In pattern, 15 sts = 4½" (11.5 cm);
   10 rows = 4¼" (10.75)
**Gauge Swatch:** 11½" wide x 4¼" long
   (29.25 cm x 10.75 cm)
Work same as Body for 10 rows: 26 dc and 12 ch-1 sps.

## INSTRUCTIONS
## Body

Ch 39.

**Row 1** (Right side)**:** Sc in 🎥 back ridge of second ch from hook and each ch across *(Fig. 1, page 29)*: 38 sc.

*Note:* Loop a short piece of yarn around any stitch to mark Row 1 as **right** side.

**Row 2:** Ch 3 (**counts as first dc, now and throughout**), turn; skip next sc, (dc, ch 1, dc) in next sc, ★ skip next 2 sc, (dc, ch 1, dc) in next sc; repeat from ★ across to last 2 sc, skip next sc, dc in last sc: 26 dc and 12 ch-1 sps.

**Row 3:** Ch 1, turn; sc in each dc and in each ch-1 sp across: 38 sc.

Repeat Rows 2 and 3 for pattern until Body measures approximately 75{90}"/190.5{228.5} cm from beginning ch, ending by working Row 3.

Finish off.

**First End Trim:** With **right** side facing and working across last row, 🎥 join yarn with sc in first sc *(see Joining With Sc, page 29)*; † skip next 2 sc, dc in next sc, (ch 1, dc in same st) twice, skip next 2 sc, sc in next sc †; repeat from † to † 2 times **more**, skip next 2 sc, dc in next sc, (ch 1, dc in same st) twice, skip next 3 sc, sc in next sc, repeat from † to † twice; finish off.

**Second End Trim:** With **right** side facing and working in 🎥 free loops of beginning ch *(Fig. 3, page 29)*, join yarn with sc in first ch; † skip next 2 chs, dc in next ch, (ch 1, dc in same st) twice, skip next 2 chs, sc in next ch †; repeat from † to † 2 times **more**, skip next 3 chs, dc in next ch, (ch 1, dc in same st) twice, skip next 2 chs, sc in next ch, repeat from † to † twice; finish off.

# Hood

Work same as Body until Hood measures approximately 19" (48.5 cm) from beginning ch, ending by working Row 3.

Finish off.

Fold Hood in half with **wrong** side together and matching last row to beginning ch. Sew ends of rows together along one side to form top seam.

Fold Body in half and mark edge at center point. Matching center of Hood to marker, pin pieces together and sew in place.

**To form Pockets:** Fold each end up 10" (25.5 cm); pin in place.

**Outer Trim:** With **right** side facing, working in ends of rows across long edge without Hood, and working through **both** layers of Pockets, join yarn with sc in first corner; sc evenly across ending in next corner; finish off.

**Inner Trim:** With **right** side facing, working in ends of rows across remaining long edge, and working through **both** layers of Pockets, join yarn with sc in first corner; sc evenly across to Hood; working in free loops of beginning ch and in sts on last row on Hood, sc in each st across; sc evenly across ending in next corner; finish off.

# BUTTON-FLAP POCKETS

 **EASY**

## SHOPPING LIST

### Yarn (Medium Weight) [4]
[3.5 ounces, 170 yards
(100 grams, 156 meters) per skein]:
☐ 6{7} skeins

### Crochet Hook
☐ Size I (5.5 mm)
**or** size needed for gauge

### Additional Supplies
☐ Yarn needle
☐ Pins
☐ 1" (25 mm) Buttons - 2
☐ Sewing needle and matching
thread

## SIZE INFORMATION
**Finished Size:**
12" (30.5 cm) wide x 22{36}"
[56{91.5} cm] long (from inside
center back neck to bottom edge)

*Size Note:* We have printed the
instructions for the sizes in different
colors to make it easier for you to find:
• Child size in Blue
• Adult size in Pink
Instructions in Black apply to both
sizes.

## GAUGE INFORMATION
In pattern, 12 sts = 4¼" (10.75 cm)
**Gauge Swatch:** 12" wide x 4" long
(30.5 cm x 10 cm)
Work same as Long Strip for 8 rows:
34 hdc.

## ─── STITCH GUIDE ───
🎥 **SINGLE CROCHET 2 TOGETHER**
*(abbreviated sc2tog)*
Pull up a loop in each of next 2 sc, YO
and draw through all 3 loops on hook
**(counts as one sc).**
🎥 **SINGLE CROCHET 3 TOGETHER**
*(abbreviated sc3tog)*
Pull up a loop in each of next 3 sc, YO
and draw through all 4 loops on hook
**(counts as one sc).**

## INSTRUCTIONS
## Long Strip
Ch 35.

**Row 1** (Right side)**:** 2 Hdc in fourth ch
from hook **(3 skipped chs count as
first hdc and one skipped ch, now
and throughout)**, (skip next ch, 2 hdc
in next ch) across to last ch, hdc in last
ch: 34 hdc.

*Note:* Loop a short piece of yarn
around any stitch to mark Row 1 as
**right** side.

**Row 2:** Ch 1, turn; sc in each hdc
across.

**Row 3:** Ch 2 **(counts as first hdc, now
and throughout)**, turn; (skip next sc,
2 hdc in next sc) across to last sc, hdc
in last sc.

Repeat Rows 2 and 3 for pattern until
Long Strip measures approximately
44{58}"/112{147.5} cm from
beginning ch, ending by working
Row 2.

Finish off.

## Short Strip
Work same as Long Strip until Short
Strip measures approximately
32{46}"/81.5{117} cm from beginning
ch, ending by working Row 2.

Finish off.

**To form Pockets:** Fold each end up
10" (25.5 cm); pin in place.

Sew each side of each Pocket.

Using Diagram as a guide for placement, working through **both** loops of each ch on Short Strip and in ends of rows on Long Strip, 📹 whipstitch *(Fig. 5a, page 30)* Strips together.

### Diagram

*Note:* Dashed lines represent top open edges of Pockets.

## Button Flap (Make 2)

Ch 8.

**Row 1** (Right side)**:** Sc in second ch from hook and in each ch across: 7 sc.

*Note:* Mark Row 1 as **right** side.

**Rows 2-8:** Ch 1, turn; sc in each sc across.

**Row 9:** Ch 1, turn; sc in first 2 sc, ch 3, skip next 3 sc **(buttonhole)**, sc in last 2 sc: 4 sc and one ch-3 sp.

**Row 10:** Ch 1, turn; sc in each sc and in each ch across: 7 sc.

**Row 11:** Ch 1, turn; sc in first sc, (sc2tog, sc in next sc) twice: 5 sc.

**Row 12:** Ch 1, turn; sc in each sc across.

**Row 13:** Ch 1, turn; sc in first sc, sc3tog, sc in last sc; finish off: 3 sc.

Sew one Button Flap centered above each Pocket.

Sew a button to each Pocket opposite the buttonhole.

## Hood

Work same as Long Strip until Hood measures approximately 20" (51 cm) from beginning ch, ending by working Row 2; finish off.

Fold Hood in half with **wrong** side together and matching last row to beginning ch. Sew ends of rows together along one side to form top seam.

Pin bottom edge of Hood along inside edge of Shawl, matching center back of Hood with Strips seam. Sew Hood to Shawl.

# DESERT STARS

■■■□ INTERMEDIATE

*Shown on page 18.*

## SHOPPING LIST

### Yarn (Medium Weight)

[1.75 ounces, 147 yards
(50 grams, 135 meters) per skein]:

☐ 5{6} skeins

### Crochet Hook

☐ Size I (5.5 mm)

or size needed for gauge

### Additional Supplies

☐ Pins

## SIZE INFORMATION

Finished Size:

12¼" wide x 55{72}" long

[31 cm x 139.5{183} cm]

*Size Note:* We have printed the
instructions for the sizes in different
colors to make it easier for you to find:

• Child size in Blue

• Adult size in Pink

Instructions in Black apply to both
sizes.

## GAUGE INFORMATION

In pattern, 6 Star Sts = 4" (10 cm);

8 rows = 3¾" (9.5 cm)

Gauge Swatch: 12" wide x 3¾" long

(30.5 cm x 9.5 cm)

Work same as Body, page 18, for 8 rows: 37 sc.

--- STITCH GUIDE ---

### 🎥 BEGINNING STAR ST

Insert hook in second ch from hook,
YO and pull up a loop, insert hook in
next ch, YO and pull up a loop, (insert
hook in Back Loop Only of **next** sc, YO
and pull up a loop) twice *(Fig. A)*, YO
and draw through all 5 loops on hook,
ch 1 to close Star St and form eyelet.

**Fig. A**

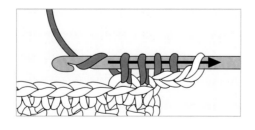

### 🎥 STAR ST

Insert hook in eyelet of last Star St
made, YO and pull up a loop, insert
hook in same sc as last Star St
completed, YO and pull up a loop,
(insert hook in Back Loop Only of
**next** sc, YO and pull up a loop) twice
*(Fig. B)*, YO and draw through all
5 loops on hook, ch 1 to close Star St
and form eyelet.

**Fig. B**

## INSTRUCTIONS
## Body

Ch 40.

**Row 1** (Right side): Working in  back ridge of ch *(Fig. 1, page 29)*, insert hook in second ch from hook, YO and pull up a loop, (insert hook in **next** ch, YO and pull up a loop) 3 times, YO and draw through all 5 loops on hook, ch 1 to close Star St and form eyelet **(first Star St made)**, ★ insert hook in eyelet of last Star St, YO and pull up a loop, insert hook in same ch as last Star St completed, YO and pull up a loop, (insert hook in **next** ch, YO and pull up a loop) twice, YO and draw through all 5 loops on hook, ch 1 to close Star St and form eyelet; repeat from ★ across to last ch, sc in last ch: 18 Star Sts.

*Note:* Loop a short piece of yarn around any stitch to mark Row 1 as **right** side.

**Row 2:** Ch 1, turn; sc in first sc and in eyelet of next Star St, 2 sc in each of next 17 eyelets, sc in last st: 37 sc.

**Row 3:** Ch 3, turn; work Beginning Star St, work Star St across to last sc, sc in **both** loops of last sc: 18 Star Sts.

Repeat Rows 2 and 3 until Body measures approximately 54¾{71¾}"/139{182} cm from beginning ch, ending by working Row 2.

Finish off.

## Pocket (Make 2)

Work same as Body until Pocket measures 10" (25.5 cm) from beginning ch, ending by working Row 2.

Finish off.

With **right** sides facing, place one Pocket on each end of Body, matching pattern and side edges, and pin in place.

## Trim

With **right** side facing and working through **both** layers along Pocket edges, join yarn with sc in any corner *(see Joining With Sc, page 29)*; 2 sc in same st, sc evenly around entire Shawl working 3 sc in each corner; join with slip st to first sc, finish off.

# STARRY NIGHT

■■□□ **EASY**

## SIZE INFORMATION

**Finished Size:**

12" (30.5 cm) wide x 22{45}"
[56{114.5} cm] long (from inside
center back neck to bottom edge)

**Size Note:** We have printed the
instructions for the sizes in different
colors to make it easier for you to find:

Child size in Blue

Adult size in Pink

Instructions in Black apply to both
sizes.

## GAUGE INFORMATION

In pattern,
   12 sts and 9 rows = 3¾" (9.5 cm)
**Gauge Swatch:**
   11¼" wide x 3¾" long
   (28.5 cm x 9.5 cm)
Work same as Long Strip for 9 rows:
36 sts.

## INSTRUCTIONS
## Long Strip

Ch 39.

**Row 1:** Hdc in third ch from hook,
★ skip next ch, (sc, hdc) in next ch;
repeat from ★ across to last 2 chs,
skip next ch, sc in last ch: 36 sts.

**Row 2:** Ch 2, turn; hdc in first sc,
★ skip next hdc, (sc, hdc) in next sc;
repeat from ★ across to last hdc, sc in
last hdc, leave turning ch unworked.

Repeat Row 2 for pattern until
Long Strip measures approximately
43{68}"/109{172.5} cm from
beginning ch.

Finish off.

## Short Strip

Work same as Long Strip until Short
Strip measures approximately
32{55}"/81.5{139.5} cm from
beginning ch.

Finish off.

**To form Pockets:** Fold each end up 10" (25.5 cm); pin in place.

Using Diagram as a guide for placement, working through **both** loops of each ch on Short Strip and in ends of rows on Long Strip, 🎥 whipstitch *(Fig. 5a, page 30)* Strips together.

## Diagram

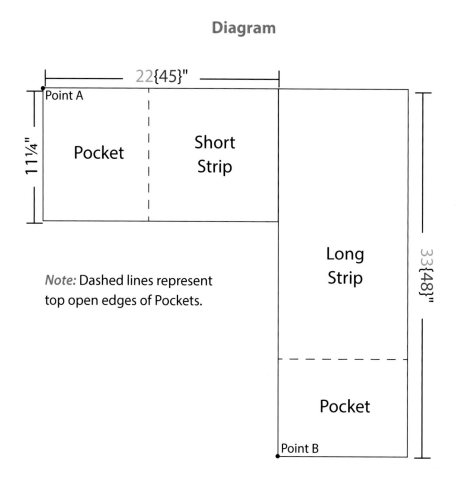

*Note:* Dashed lines represent top open edges of Pockets.

## Trim

**Row 1:** Working across outer long edge and Pocket away from you, 🎥 join yarn with sc at Point A on Diagram *(see Joining With Sc, page 29)*; evenly space an odd number of sc across to the bottom corner of Second Pocket.

**Row 2:** Ch 2, turn; hdc in first sc, ★ skip next sc, (sc, hdc) in next sc; repeat from ★ across to last 2 sc, skip next sc, sc in last sc; finish off.

Repeat for inner long edge, join yarn at Point B on Diagram.

# BUTTON-ON HOODY

## SHOPPING LIST

### Yarn (Medium Weight)

**Child{Doll} Size**

[3.5 ounces, 170 yards
(100 grams, 156 meters) per skein]:

☐  4{1} skein(s)

**Adult Size**

[5 ounces, 256 yards
(141 grams, 234 meters) per skein]:

☐  4 skeins

### Crochet Hook

☐  Size H (5 mm)

   **or** size needed for gauge

### Additional Supplies

☐  Yarn needle

☐  ¾" (19 mm) Buttons - 5{5-0}

☐  Sewing needle and matching
   thread

## SIZE INFORMATION

**Finished Size:**

   11{11-3}" wide x 55{71-17½}" long
   [28{28-7.5} cm x
   139.5{180.5-44.5} cm]

*Size Note:* We have printed the
instructions for the sizes in different
colors to make it easier for you to find:

• Child size in Blue

• Adult size in Pink

• Doll size in Green

Instructions in Black apply to all sizes.

## GAUGE INFORMATION

In pattern,

   2 repeats and 6 rows = 4" (10 cm)

**Gauge Swatch:** 11" wide x 4" long

   (28 cm x 10 cm)

Work same as Body for 6 rows: 29 dc
and 5 ch-2 sps.

## —— STITCH GUIDE ——

**FOUNDATION SINGLE CROCHET**
   *(abbreviated fsc)*

Ch 2, insert hook in second ch from
hook, YO and pull up a loop, YO and
draw through one loop on hook
(**ch made**), YO and draw through
both loops on hook (**first fsc made**),
★ insert hook in ch at base of last
fsc made, YO and pull up a loop, YO
and draw through one loop on hook
(**ch made**), YO and draw through both
loops on hook (**fsc made**); repeat
from ★ for each additional fsc.

## INSTRUCTIONS (For Child and Adult Size ONLY)
## Body

**Row 1** (Right side)**:** Work 34 fsc.

*Note:* Loop a short piece of yarn
around any stitch to mark Row 1 as
**right** side.

**Row 2:** Ch 3 (**counts as first dc, now
and throughout**), turn; dc in next
2 fsc, (dc, ch 2, dc) in next fsc, ★ skip
next 2 fsc, dc in next 3 fsc, (dc, ch 2,
dc) in next fsc; repeat from ★ across
to last 6 fsc, skip next 2 fsc, dc in last
4 fsc: 29 dc and 5 ch-2 sps.

**Row 3:** Ch 3, turn; dc in next 2 dc, (dc,
ch 2, dc) in next dc, skip next dc and
next ch-2 sp, ★ dc in next 3 dc, (dc,
ch 2, dc) in next dc, skip next dc and
next ch-2 sp; repeat from ★ across to
last 4 dc, dc in last 4 dc.

Repeat Row 3 for pattern until
piece measures approximately
74¾{90¾}"/190{230.5} cm from
bottom edge, ending by working a
**wrong** side row.

**Last Row:** Ch 1, turn; sc in each dc
and in each ch across; finish off: 39 sc.

**To form Pockets:** Fold each end up
10" (25.5 cm); pin in place.

Sew each side of each Pocket.

# Hood

Work same as Body until piece measures approximately 19¾" (50 cm) from bottom edge, ending by working a **right** side row.

**Last Row:** Ch 1, turn; sc in each dc and in each ch across; finish off: 39 sc.

**Top Trim:** With **right** side facing, working in end of rows across one long edge,  join yarn with sc in first row *(see Joining With Sc, page 29)*; work 60 sc evenly spaced across; finish off leaving a long end for sewing: 61 sc.

Fold Hood in half along Top Trim and whipstitch *(Fig. 5a, page 30)* top seam of Hood together.

**Front Trim:** With **right** side facing, working in sts of last row and in free loops at bottom of Row 1 *(Fig. 3, page 29)*, join yarn with sc in first st; work 73 sc evenly spaced across; finish off: 74 sc.

# Buttonhole Band

**Row 1:** With **right** side facing, working in end of rows across remaining long edge, join yarn with sc in first row; work 60 sc evenly spaced across: 61 sc.

**Row 2:** Ch 1, turn; sc in first 2 sc, ch 1 (**buttonhole made**), ★ skip next sc, sc in next 13 sc, ch 1 (**buttonhole made**); repeat from ★ across to last 3 sc, skip next sc, sc in last 2 sc: 56 sc and 5 buttonholes.

**Row 3:** Ch 1, turn; sc in each sc and in each ch across; finish off: 61 sc.

Matching center of Buttonhole Band on Hood to **wrong** side of center on Body, mark placement of buttons.

Sew buttons to **wrong** side of Body.

Button Hood to Body.

## INSTRUCTIONS (For Doll Size ONLY)

### Body

**Row 1** (Right side)**:** Work 10 fsc.

*Note:* Loop a short piece of yarn around any stitch to mark Row 1 as **right** side.

**Row 2:** Ch 3 **(counts as first dc, now and throughout)**, turn; dc in next 2 fsc, (dc, ch 2, dc) in next fsc, skip next 2 fsc, dc in last 4 fsc: 9 dc and one ch-2 sp.

**Row 3:** Ch 3, turn; dc in next 2 dc, (dc, ch 2, dc) in next dc, skip next dc and next ch-2 sp, dc in last 4 dc.

Repeat Row 3 until piece measures approximately 21¼" (54 cm) from bottom edge, ending by working a **wrong** side row.

**Last Row:** Ch 1, turn; sc in each dc and in each ch across; finish off: 11 sc.

**To form Pocket:** Fold each end up 2" (5 cm); pin in place.

Sew each side of each Pocket.

### Hood

**Row 1** (Right side)**:** Work 16 fsc.

*Note:* Mark Row 1 as **right** side.

**Row 2:** Ch 3 **(counts as first dc, now and throughout)**, turn; dc in next 2 fsc, (dc, ch 2, dc) in next fsc, skip next 2 fsc, dc in next 3 fsc, (dc, ch 2, dc) in next fsc skip next 2 fsc, dc in last 4 fsc: 14 dc and 2 ch-2 sps.

**Row 3:** Ch 3, turn; dc in next 2 dc, (dc, ch 2, dc) in next dc, skip next dc and next ch-2 sp, dc in next 3 dc, (dc, ch 2, dc) in next dc, skip next dc and next ch-2 sp, dc in last 4 dc.

Repeat Row 3 until piece measures approximately 8¾" (22 cm) from bottom edge, ending by working a **right** side row.

**Last Row:** Ch 1, turn; sc in each dc and in each ch across; finish off: 18 sc.

**Top Trim:** With **right** side facing, working in ends of rows across one long edge, 🎥 join yarn with sc in first row *(see Joining With Sc, page 29)*; work 24 sc evenly spaced across; finish off leaving a long end for sewing: 25 sc.

Fold Hood in half along Top Trim and 🎥 whipstitch *(Fig. 5a, page 30)* top seam of Hood together.

**Front Trim:** With **right** side facing, working in sts of last row and in 🎥 free loops at bottom of Row 1 *(Fig. 3, page 29)*, join Blue with sc in first sc; work 37 sc evenly spaced across; finish off: 38 sc.

Fold Body in half and mark edge at center point. Matching center of Hood to marker, pin pieces together. Sew in place.

# SHADOW POCKETS

 **EASY**

*Shown on page 27.*

## SIZE INFORMATION

**Finished Size:**

11½{11½-3}" [29{29-7.5} cm] wide x
22{35-8}" [56{89-20.5} cm] long
(from inside center back neck to
bottom edge)

*Size Note:* We have printed the
instructions for the sizes in different
colors to make it easier for you to find:

Child size in Blue

Adult size in Pink

Doll size in Green

Instructions in Black apply to all sizes.

## GAUGE INFORMATION

In pattern, 14 sts = 4" (10 cm);
  16 rows = 3¾" (9.5 cm)

**Gauge Swatch:** 11½" wide x 3¾" long
  (29.25 cm x 9.5 cm)

Work same as Long Strip for 16 rows:
20 hdc and 20 slip sts.

## ——— STITCH GUIDE ———

🎥 **FOUNDATION SINGLE CROCHET**
  *(abbreviated fsc)*

Ch 2, insert hook in second ch from
hook, YO and pull up a loop, YO and
draw through one loop on hook
(**ch made**), YO and draw through
both loops on hook (**first fsc made**),
★ insert hook in ch at base of last
fsc made, YO and pull up a loop, YO
and draw through one loop on hook
(**ch made**), YO and draw through both
loops on hook (**fsc made**); repeat
from ★ for each additional fsc.

## INSTRUCTIONS
## Long Strip

**Row 1** (Right side)**:** With
Dk Rose{Blue-Dk Rose}, work
40{40-10} fsc.

*Note:* Loop a short piece of yarn
around any stitch to mark Row 1 as
**right** side.

**Row 2:** Ch 2, turn; hdc in first fsc,
slip st in next fsc, (hdc in next fsc,
slip st in next fsc) across: 20{20-5} hdc
and 20{20-5} slip sts.

**Row 3:** Ch 2, turn; hdc in first slip st,
slip st in next hdc, (hdc in next slip st,
slip st in next hdc) across.

Repeat Row 3 for pattern until
Long Strip measures approximately
33½{46½-11}"/85{118-28} cm from
bottom edge, ending by working a
**right** side row.

Finish off.

## Short Strip

Work same as Long Strip until
Short Strip measures approximately
22{35-8}"/56{89-20.5} cm from
bottom edge, ending by working a
**right** side row.

Finish off.

Using Diagram as a guide for placement and with Dk Rose {Blue-Dk Rose}, working through **both** loops of each ch on Short Strip and in ends of rows on Long Strip, 🎥 whipstitch *(Fig. 5a, page 30)* Strips together.

### Diagram

22{35-8}"

11½{11½-3}"

Pocket

Short Strip

Long Strip

33½{46½-11}"

Pocket

*Note:* Dashed lines represent top open edges of Pockets.

## Pocket (Make 2)

Row 1 (Right side): **With** Rose{Dk Blue-Rose}, **work** 30{30-8} fsc.

*Note:* Mark Row 1 as **right** side.

Row 2: Ch 2, turn; hdc in first fsc, slip st in next fsc, (hdc in next fsc, slip st in next fsc) across: 15{15-4} hdc and 15{15-4} slip sts.

Row 3: Ch 2, turn; hdc in first slip st, slip st in next hdc, (hdc in next slip st, slip st in next hdc) across.

Repeat Row 3 until Pocket measures approximately 10{10-2}"/25.5{25.5-5} cm from bottom edge, ending by working a **right** side row.

Finish off.

Using photo as a guide for placement, place bottom edge of each Pocket approximately ¼" (6 mm) from bottom edge of the Strip centering Pocket across the width. Pin the Pockets in place. With Rose{Dk Blue-Rose}, sew around three sides of each Pocket, leaving top edge of Pocket open.

# GENERAL INSTRUCTIONS

## ABBREVIATIONS

| | |
|---|---|
| ch(s) | chain(s) |
| cm | centimeters |
| dc | double crochet(s) |
| fsc | foundation single crochet(s) |
| hdc | half double crochet(s) |
| mm | millimeters |
| Rnd(s) | Round(s) |
| sc | single crochet(s) |
| sc2tog | single crochet 2 together |
| sc3tog | single crochet 3 together |
| sp(s) | space(s) |
| st(s) | stitch(es) |
| YO | yarn over |

## SYMBOLS & TERMS

★ — work instructions following ★ as many **more** times as indicated in addition to the first time.

† to † — work all instructions from first † to second † **as many** times as specified.

( ) or [ ] — work enclosed instructions **as many** times as specified by the number immediately following **or** work all enclosed instructions in the stitch or space indicated **or** contains explanatory remarks.

colon (:) — the number(s) given after a colon at the end of a row or round denote(s) the number of stitches or spaces you should have on that row or round.

## GAUGE

Exact gauge is **essential** for proper size. Before beginning your project, make the sample swatch given in the individual instructions in the yarn and hook specified. After completing the swatch, measure it, counting your stitches and rows carefully. If your swatch is larger or smaller than specified, **make another, changing hook size to get the correct gauge**. Keep trying until you find the size hook that will give you the specified gauge.

| CROCHET TERMINOLOGY | |
|---|---|
| **UNITED STATES** | **INTERNATIONAL** |
| slip stitch (slip st) | = single crochet (sc) |
| single crochet (sc) | = double crochet (dc) |
| half double crochet (hdc) | = half treble crochet (htr) |
| double crochet (dc) | = treble crochet (tr) |
| treble crochet (tr) | = double treble crochet (dtr) |
| double treble crochet (dtr) | = triple treble crochet (ttr) |
| triple treble crochet (tr tr) | = quadruple treble crochet (qtr) |
| skip | = miss |

| Yarn Weight Symbol & Names | LACE 0 | SUPER FINE 1 | FINE 2 | LIGHT 3 | MEDIUM 4 | BULKY 5 | SUPER BULKY 6 |
|---|---|---|---|---|---|---|---|
| Type of Yarns in Category | Fingering, 10-count crochet thread | Sock, Fingering Baby | Sport, Baby | DK, Light Worsted | Worsted, Afghan, Aran | Chunky, Craft, Rug | Bulky, Roving |
| Crochet Gauge* Ranges in Single Crochet to 4" (10 cm) | 32-42 double crochets** | 21-32 sts | 16-20 sts | 12-17 sts | 11-14 sts | 8-11 sts | 5-9 sts |
| Advised Hook Size Range | Steel*** 6,7,8 Regular hook B-1 | B-1 to E-4 | E-4 to 7 | 7 to I-9 | I-9 to K-10½ | K-10½ to M/N-13 | M/N-13 and larger |

*GUIDELINES ONLY: The chart above reflects the most commonly used gauges and hook sizes for specific yarn categories.

** Lace weight yarns are usually crocheted on larger-size hooks to create lacy openwork patterns. Accordingly, a gauge range is difficult to determine. Always follow the gauge stated in your pattern.

*** Steel crochet hooks are sized differently from regular hooks—the higher the number the smaller the hook, which is the reverse of regular hook sizing.

| | | | |
|---|---|---|---|
| ◖□□□ BEGINNER | Projects for first-time crocheters using basic stitches. Minimal shaping. | | |
| ◖■□□ EASY | Projects using yarn with basic stitches, repetitive stitch patterns, simple color changes, and simple shaping and finishing. | | |
| ◖■■□ INTERMEDIATE | Projects using a variety of techniques, such as basic lace patterns or color patterns, mid-level shaping and finishing. | | |
| ◖■■■ EXPERIENCED | Projects with intricate stitch patterns, techniques and dimension, such as non-repeating patterns, multi-color techniques, fine threads, small hooks, detailed shaping and refined finishing. | | |

| CROCHET HOOKS | | | | | | | | | | | | | | | | | |
|---|---|---|---|---|---|---|---|---|---|---|---|---|---|---|---|---|---|
| U.S. | B-1 | C-2 | D-3 | E-4 | F-5 | G-6 | 7 | H-8 | I-9 | J-10 | K-10½ | L-11 | M/N-13 | N/P-15 | P/Q | Q | S |
| Metric - mm | 2.25 | 2.75 | 3.25 | 3.5 | 3.75 | 4 | 4.5 | 5 | 5.5 | 6 | 6.5 | 8 | 9 | 10 | 15 | 16 | 19 |

# JOINING WITH SC

When instructed to join with a sc, begin with a slip knot on hook. Insert hook in stitch or space indicated, YO and pull up a loop, YO and draw through both loops on hook.

# JOINING WITH DC

When instructed to join with a dc, begin with a slip knot on hook. YO, holding loop on hook, insert hook in stitch or space indicated, YO and pull up a loop (3 loops on hook), (YO and draw through both loops on hook) twice.

# BACK RIDGE

Work only in loop(s) indicated by arrows (Fig. 1).

Fig. 1

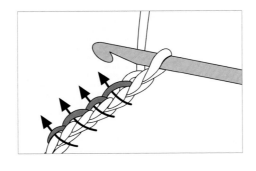

# BACK LOOPS ONLY

Work only in loop(s) indicated by arrow (Fig. 2).

Fig. 2

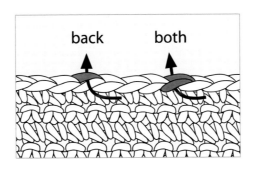

# FREE LOOPS

When instructed to work in free loops of a chain, work in loop indicated by arrow (Fig. 3).

Fig. 3

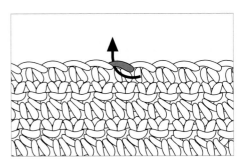

## WORKING IN SPACE BEFORE A STITCH

When instructed to work in space **before** a stitch or in spaces **between** stitches, insert hook in space indicated by arrow *(Fig. 4)*.

## WHIPSTITCH

Place two pieces with **wrong** sides together. Sew through both pieces once to secure the beginning of the seam, leaving an ample yarn end to weave in later. Working through **both** loops of **each** stitch on **both** pieces or through **inside** loops of **both** pieces, insert the needle from **front** to **back** through first stitch and pull yarn through *(Fig. 5a or 5b)*, ★ insert the needle from **front** to **back** through next stitch and pull yarn through; repeat from ★ across.

Fig. 4

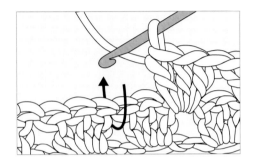

Fig. 5a

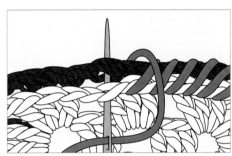

Fig. 5b

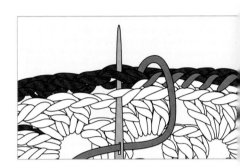

## REVERSE SC

Working from **left** to **right**, ★ insert hook in st or sp to right of hook *(Fig. 6a)*, YO and draw through, under and to the left of loop on hook (2 loops on hook) *(Fig. 6b)*, YO and draw through both loops on hook *(Fig. 6c)* (reverse sc made, *Fig. 6d*); repeat from ★ around.

Fig. 6a

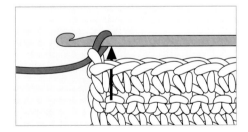

Fig. 6b

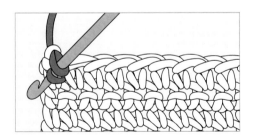

Fig. 6c

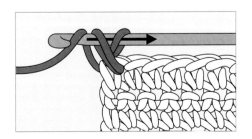

Fig. 6d

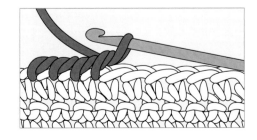

# YARN INFORMATION

The Shawls in this book were made using Medium Weight yarn. Any brand of Medium Weight yarn may be used. It is best to refer to the yardage/meters when determining how many balls or skeins to purchase. Remember, to arrive at the finished size, it is the GAUGE/TENSION that is important, not the brand of yarn.

For your convenience, listed below are the specific yarns used to create our photography models.

### COASTAL TIDE

*Red Heart® Boutique Unforgettable®*
 #3960 Tidal

### PERKY PATCHES

*Lion Brand® Vanna's Choice®*
Dk Gold - #130 Honey
Red - #133 Brick
Rust - #135 Rust
Beige - #123 Beige
Gold - #158 Mustard

### GRANNY POCKETS

*Lion Brand® Heartland®*
Grey - #350 Mount Rainer Tweed
Rust - #135 Yosemite

### HOODED COMFY

*Lion Brand® Cotton-Ease®*
#122 Taupe

### BUTTON-FLAP POCKETS

*Lion Brand® Vanna's Choice®*
#107 Sapphire

### DESERT STARS

*Lion Brand® Amazing®*
#211 Strawberry Fields

### STARRY NIGHT

*Red Heart® Boutique Midnight®*
#9803 Borealis

### BUTTON-ON HOODY

**Child and Doll Sizes:**
*Lion Brand® Vanna's Choice®*
#102 Aqua
**Adult Size:**
*Red Heart® Soft®*
#9779 Berry

### SHADOW POCKETS

*Lion Brand® Wool-Ease®*
**Child and Doll Sizes:**
Dk Rose - #139 Dark Rose Heather
Rose - #140 Rose Heather
**Adult Size:**
Blue -  #114 Denim
DK Blue - #194 Denim Twist

# MEET THE DESIGNER

Karen Whooley says childhood crochet lessons from her Italian grandmother helped her become the designer that she is today. "She didn't speak English, so she didn't know how to read an American pattern," Karen explains. "She taught me how to 'read the pictures' in order to create the item in the book. Because of this, I tended to make patterns differently than they were written, because many times I had to figure out how it was put together. So technically I consider myself a designer from the age of 7!"

Karen's designs for knitting, crochet, and the Knook have been published in numerous books and magazines, and she teaches worldwide at special events and in classes at guilds, yarn shops, and online. A self-described "computer geek at heart," she does her own web design and marketing for her indie pattern line at KRWknitwear.com.

Other Leisure Arts books featuring Karen's designs include *Easy Knit Projects Using the Knook for Kids, Fair Isle for Family, Shower of Cables, I Can't Believe I'm Crocheting Socks, Crochet Scarves and Cowls,* and *Knit Scarves and Cowls.*

Besides knitting and crocheting, she loves to spend time with her husband and teenaged children, watch football, work in her garden, and spin yarn.

We have made every effort to ensure that these instructions are accurate and complete. We cannot, however, be responsible for human error, typographical mistakes, or variations in individual work.

Production Team: Instructional/Technical Editor - Lois J. Long; Editorial Writer - Susan Frantz Wiles; Senior Graphic Artist - Lora Puls; Graphic Artist - Cailen Cochran; Photo Stylist - Lori Wenger; and Photographer - Jason Masters.

Items made and instructions tested by Melanie Clark, Lisa Chimento, Amy Curtin, Nancy Kolton, Kim Kotary, Jennifer Milton, Margaret Taverner, Karen Taylor, Karen Whooley, and Ashley Young.